USBORNE

Friendship

SURVIVAL GUIDE

Expert advice from

Dr Angharad Rudkin
Clinical Psychologist

Usborne Quicklinks

The internet is a great source of information, but it's very important to know which sites you can trust.

We have selected some useful websites to supplement the information in this book and these are available at **Usborne Quicklinks**. Here you can find more advice about friends and friendship, bullying and mental health, as well as where to go for help.

For links to all these sites, go to:
usborne.com/Quicklinks
and type in the title of this book
or scan the QR code below.

Please follow the internet safety guidelines at Usborne Quicklinks. Children should be supervised online.

USBORNE

Friendship

SURVIVAL GUIDE

Caroline Young

Designed by
Stephanie Jeffries

Illustrated by
The Boy Fitz Hammond
and Helen Lang

Edited by
Felicity Brooks

Introduction

'Friendship' is such a warm, fuzzy word, isn't it? It makes you think of having fun, feeling safe and hanging out with mates you trust, who always have your back. Awww. Yes, friendship can be fabulous, but when things go wrong, and you don't feel a) safe, b) warm or c) fuzzy, you might need some help. Luckily, you've found this book.

Few things are perfect (not even your uber-filtered profile pic – more about that later). Most things have a good side and a not-so-good side, and friendship is no different. The key is to know what makes a good friendship, and how to survive the hiccups in yours. This book is packed with survival tactics so that when problems happen, and they will, you know how to cope.

Friends are some of the most important people in our lives, so it's worth knowing how to choose them, and keep them. Time to read on...

Contents

FRIENDSHIP

My mission —
to be a SUPER
friend!

SWOOSH

CHAPTER ONE

All about friends

So what IS a friend – and why do we need them?

You are one hundred per cent unique, a complete one-off, an individual: there is **nobody** exactly like you anywhere else in the whole world. Sure, you'll meet many, many people during your lifetime, and some of them will love you, some of them you'll love, and quite of few of them you won't like AT ALL, but, basically, you're on your own in life and nobody can actually get inside your skin. But don't panic! It's not as grim as it sounds.

Luckily, people realized a long time ago that being on your own in the world was not much fun and that life was much easier (and safer) if they looked out for each other. They lived in communities, found food and shelter together, formed family groups and cared about each other.

People realized that they *needed* other people, and we still do today (even though our reasons might be a little less urgent than imminent death-by-mammoth).

Apart from our family, many of the close relationships we form are with people we call our **friends**. A simple-sounding word, but have you ever thought about what it actually *means*? Here's a pretty good definition:

friend

someone who genuinely likes you for who you are but is not a member of your family.

You're the BEST!

In our busy lives, a friend is much more than someone who keeps an eye out for danger. They are someone whose company you enjoy, who likes at least some of the things you like, who will support you if you're having a tough time, and probably laughs at the same silly things as you do.

Who wouldn't want THAT in their lives?

What matters to me?

Let's try a little experiment... Quickly jot down* the ten most important things in your life on a piece of paper. It won't be exactly like this one, but you get the idea. Be **completely honest**, please:

- [ ] My family
- [ ] Freddie, my dog
- [ ] My phone
- [ ] Gaming
- [ ] Getting an A in my maths exam
- [ ] My friends
- [ ] My social media followers/profile
- [ ] My PRIVATE bedroom
- [ ] The local donkey sanctuary
- [ ] Streaming THAT new show

Listed your ten things? Well, that was the easy part.

*You'll find useful blank pages at the back of the book.

Now it's time to THINK!

Put a number next to each one, with $\boxed{1}$ as 'the most important thing', down to number $\boxed{10}$, at the bottom of your list. So, were 'friends' up there in your top five? If so, absolutely no surprises there. (If not, you are one exceptional young

person.) Friends are probably more important than most other things to you right now – even donkeys. In fact, researchers have found that, for young people, friends are as vital as parents are to a newborn baby. You really, *really* need them in your life.

We all need friends!

Before we move on, you'll probably notice that 'my social media followers/profile' was on the list on page 14. Was it on your list, too? Social media is a great way of staying in touch with people, but it has changed the meaning of 'friends' in some ways, which can cause problems.

> I have hundreds of friends, but nobody to talk to.

You'll find lots more about how social media can affect friendships, how to keep it in check, and in perspective, in Chapter 8.

Why are friends important?

Now that we know our friends are pretty important, let's have a closer look at *why*. We're back to that 'warm, fuzzy feeling' again.

Friends should make us **feel good** when we spend time with them, even if we're doing simple things like chatting after school or listening to music together. The key to a good friendship is that you:

are comfortable in each other's company

care about each other's feelings

want to spend time together

Not all friendships are the same, though. Some friends you will feel really close to, and trust with your deepest, darkest secrets (or let them borrow your cool new jacket). Others you might only see occasionally, meet on holiday, or play with in the same team every weekend. You might have some you don't see often at all, but know they're out there (and that's when social media can be a **good** thing). Aim for a wide selection of friends if you can.

What friends do

Doing things with other people is a great way of getting to know them better. So what do you do with *your* friends that brings you closer together? Here are some possibilities, but there are lots, lots more:

• share adventures

• play online and offline games

• play a sport together

- solve problems
- relax
- cook and share a meal
- watch a movie together

Sometimes, all you want to do with your friends is **be** with them. Feeling relaxed in their company is a big part of why friendship is so good for your wellbeing.

Sharing and caring

Enjoying doing stuff with your friends is important, but you don't need to be clones and do EXACTLY what they do. As long as you enjoy enough of the same kinds of things, a friendship can thrive. To see how much you and your friends share, try drawing a diagram like this on a sheet of paper and put your name next to one circle, and perhaps one of your closest friends near the other. Now put all the things you BOTH like in the middle, where the two circles overlap.

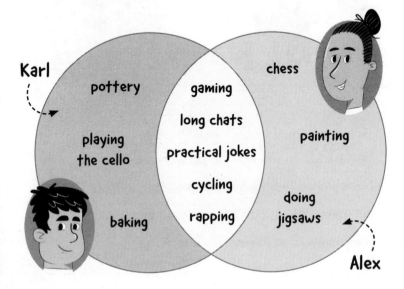

Karl

pottery

playing
the cello

baking

gaming

long chats

practical jokes

cycling

rapping

chess

painting

doing
jigsaws

Alex

Did you find that you and that friend share a lot more than you realized? That's great – it's like a solid foundation beneath your friendship. But there's much more to the whole business of friendship than just doing fun stuff together, isn't there?

Sometimes, life is far from fun and that's when you need different things from your mates, and they might need different things from you.

Being a friend means looking out for someone else and letting them know you care. Here are some ways you might do that, but there are lots more:

- **comfort them if they're sad**
- **stick up for them**
- **listen to, and respect, their views**
- **accept it if they need some space...**

...and sometimes, they might. Friendship is a complicated thing and there's a lot of give and take involved. (You'll find lots more about how to get through the tricky times in a friendship in Chapter 9 of this book.)

And finally, family

Now you may not want to hear this (as your Aunty Dorothy has probably been whispering it in your ear your whole life) but your family or carers are vital to your wellbeing, too.

In fact, in what they do for you, they are probably the closest friends you will ever have, even though the definition of a 'friend' actually excludes them. You'll fall out, shut them out, put them down to your mates and sometimes wish you had an entirely different one, but your family are the friends you **can't** choose, and always will be.

Remember the list of 'ways to show you care' on the opposite page? Ring any bells when you think about your family? Yep, they can cause problems, let you down and deeply embarrass you, but if you're lucky, they care about you more than any friend you will ever have.

CHAPTER TWO

Good friends
(and how to be one)

Hopefully, after reading the first chapter, you have a good idea of what friends are, and why you need them in your life. Next, we'll look at your side of the deal, and how to be a good friend yourself. It may sound simple enough (basically 'be nice to people') but it's much more than that. Research shows that people who **are** good friends, have a much better chance of **having** some themselves.

FRIEND or FLAKE ?

Let's begin with a quick quiz. Choose **one** (yes, only ONE, which you may find tricky!) of the four possible answers to these three questions:

Q1 – A party is coming up and your friend is planning to wear something you know they'll get teased about. **WHAT DO YOU DO?**

a) Let them. It's their choice (but avoid them at the party).

b) Tell them straight to wear something else, and why.

c) Respect their choice, but tell them they'll get ribbed.

d) Gently offer some alternative outfit suggestions.

What do you think of this one? I LOVE it!

Q2 – It's late, and one of your friends is panicking about school work that's due in tomorrow. You're tired, but they need to talk. **WHAT DO YOU DO?**

a) Suggest they ring someone else. You're too tired now.

b) Tell them to just get on with it, as you did.

c) Make yourself a cuppa, get comfy and call them.

d) Suggest they get some sleep and try again tomorrow.

Q3 – A friend has told you something worrying, but asked you not to tell anyone else. **WHAT DO YOU DO?**

a) Forget it. You have your own problems.

b) Tell your friend you feel you have to tell your parents.

c) Tell your friend that you'll go with them to tell someone they trust.

d) Tell someone you trust, in absolute confidence, and then decide what to do to help your friend together.

Turn the page to see what your answers reveal.

Did you struggle to choose only one answer? Be honest, folks! Sometimes, being a good friend is not completely straightforward, is it? That old saying '**A friend in need is a friend indeed**' is pretty accurate, because when you're 'in need' is the time you rely on your friends most.

If you choose the c) and d) answers,

well done

– you have a sound idea of what it takes to be a friend.

If you chose the a) or b) answers... well, that's OK, but perhaps it's time to have a look at yourself and think how you could be a better friend.

It's easy when you know how – this book is here to help.

Three key qualities

The quiz on pages 26 and 27 was designed to show you three key qualities you need if you want to be a good friend:

1 **Respect**

2 **Kindness**

3 **Loyalty**

You'll remember from Chapter 1 that you also need to enjoy doing things together, but good, solid friendships are built on these three key qualities. And they need them ALL to survive and thrive.

We're the Dream Team!

There's one more quality that's very important in friendship – **honesty**.

But if you look back at the a) and b) quiz answers, you'll see that they are one hundred per cent **honest**, but they aren't **kind**, are they? It's always best, if you possibly can, to listen, and then find a kind way of helping or advising a friend. Then, they are more likely to do the same for you when you need them to.

Understanding how another person might feel is called **empathy** and it's another key ingredient in a successful friendship.

You can read more about listening to friends, and empathy, in Chapter 4.

Happy helpers

Researchers have found that we get a 'helper's high' if we do something kind for someone else. You could try it, and see if it makes you feel good.

Can you think of something small you could do to help somebody you know? Perhaps an elderly neighbour can't mow their lawn easily? Could you help load the dishwasher or sort the washing? Do you think your mate might need a hand to get to the next level of that game he started playing?

Something that seems almost nothing to you could make a real difference to someone else.

This is actually making me feel pretty good.

What about you?

Just by reading this book, you're really refining your qualities as a friend, and thinking about how to support others, which is great. Now it's time to think about YOURSELF a little. Does that sound a bit weird/selfish/irrelevant? Well, it's not. It's important both to **know** and to **like** yourself: if you do, it's much easier for others to like you too! It's time to discover what makes you, YOU.

Quickly jot down four random facts about yourself:

I am rubbish at science.
Booooo
I like playing football.
I can knit.
I love fantasy stories and cosplay.

Now it might get trickier...

Jot down four **positive** things about yourself. Here are some ideas to start you thinking:

Yes, FOUR!

I help my Mum look after my little brother.

I can make people laugh.

I care about the environment.

I try to eat fruit and vegetables every day.

Perhaps you can think of *more* than four, you legend!

Bad... or good?

It's all too easy to want to be perfect, and beat yourself up if you lose your cool/have an enormous zit/have a **very** bad hair day.

Not even close. Sigh.

Experts sometimes call that little voice inside your head (the one that is constantly reminding you of how bad things are) your 'inner critic'.

To be a friend to someone else, it's worth trying to quieten that voice as much as you can, because it can give you a very negative, inaccurate view of the world, and of people. Not good. Try this next activity to show you how powerful an 'inner critic' can be.

Write down three things that happened in the past week that bothered you, didn't go well or made you feel BAD. It might be these sort of things:

I wasn't picked for the hockey team.

I didn't get a good mark for my History test.

My hair looked like a bird's nest all day.

Now, write down three things in the past week that went **well** (or at least OK). They might be simple things, like these, but you MUST write three:

I got to sit next to Jed in Geography.

I sold something online so I can afford those boots.

We watched an interesting film in our English lesson.

Was it more difficult to write the **positive** things than the **negative** ones? If it was, you can see how loud that 'inner critic' can be. Often, the way we look at things, and at people, can change our mood, making us a positive person, rather than one who always focuses on the downsides of life (and there will always be some, every single day!).

Try as hard as you can to see the good things about yourself, about others, and about the world. It can take a bit of practice, but it can be life-changing.

Core values

Knowing yourself, and recognizing that you aren't perfect, is not easy, but it's vital. Remember that there are some *seriously good things* about you (check back at your list): it may help you feel confident in what you offer as a friend.

At the heart of all of us, whether they're hidden away or clear to all, are what are sometimes called '**core values**'. These might include...

adventure fairness courage
integrity patience
fitness kindness generosity

Put simply, these are the things that matter to us, and are at the heart of the way we'd like to live our lives. If you want to be a good friend and to have good friends, it helps to work out what your core values are. It's easier than it sounds, honestly!

Here are four possibilities, but when you write your list, it might be completely different (and you might have more than four possibilities. There's no limit.):

* Treat other people as I want to be treated

* Listen to other peoples' views
  (even if I don't share them)

* Don't give up if something is difficult

* Be loyal to my friends

Hopefully, you feel quite proud of what you've just written. You might never have thought about it until now, but your list will show the 'real' you, the one under the front we all put up at times, when we're with other people.

If you can show these values in everything you do, the friends you make will see it and appreciate it. Any friend worth having will want to know the REAL you, not a fake, filtered version.

Be the real deal, and remember to:

STAY
TRUE
TO
YOU!

CHAPTER THREE

Making friends
(and how to do it)

'Making friends' sounds so easy, doesn't it?
You spot someone who seems nice, you chat,
you 'click' and the rest is history. But let's be honest
here: for a lot of us, getting to know someone new
isn't easy at all. In fact, it can be pretty scary. Even
people who seem super-confident on the outside
can be painfully shy on the inside. If you'd like
a few tips on friend-making, read on...

First impressions

The way you come across to someone is important, so it's a good idea to think about how you introduce yourself. First impressions are key, as we all make decisions about people we meet very quickly. You may not believe it, but we send 'signals' to others without even realizing we're doing it. Take a look at these twins:

Which one would you like to get to know?

So, did you choose Sirajul?

If you did, you probably didn't need to think about it much, because the 'signals' you picked up on were very clear ones:

- he's smiling
- he's looking at you, making eye-contact
- his face and posture look welcoming, as if he wants to meet you
- he's greeting you in a warm way

Basically, he looks **friendly**, doesn't he?

Little things make a big, big difference in how other people see you, so you need to send out those signals too, loud and clear.

(Oh, and if you picked Dev, that's OK, but you may find making friends harder than it needs to be.)

Shyness busters

OK, all good stuff, but what if you still feel too shy to say anything? Don't worry – you are not alone. Talking to someone new can feel like a big leap into the unknown. Try these quick tips to give you a bit of *oomph*:

1 Squeeze something in your pocket, like a pebble or a key. Weirdly, this can help focus some of your nerves on that thing, and nothing else.

2 Take a few (quiet) slow, deep breaths before you speak. Feel your body calming and your tummy relaxing.

Ahhhhhhhhhhhhh.

3 Remember that the other person is just like you, with their fair share of faults and problems, but lots to offer, as well.

4 Remember that perhaps, just perhaps, the other person is feeling shy too and hoping YOU will make the first move.

5 Finally, what's the worst thing that can happen? Exactly. The world won't end and you will eat dinner tonight.

It can feel tricky to approach someone you don't know yet, and begin to get to know them, but if you don't try, you'll never succeed! Even super-confident-seeming celebs say that they often feel anxious about meeting new people. It's natural. Be yourself, and believe you're worth getting to know.

Go you!

THE
ME, ME, ME!
QUIZ

There's another key factor in how you interact with others – whether you **listen**. There's more about this on pages 58 and 59, but let's see how well you do at letting others express their thoughts and feelings.

Answer these questions as honestly as you can, without over-thinking it. Choose **one** answer:

Q1 – If you were talking to someone who plays in a football team and goes on about it ALL THE TIME, which one of these things would you say?

a) "Tell me all about the match you played last night."

b) "Please, no more about football!"

c) "I hear the team's doing well. What was the final score?"

Q2 – *Someone won't let you say what you want to without interrupting. What do you say to them?*

a) "Your interruptions are SO annoying."

b) You say nothing. There's no point, as they won't listen.

c) "Hey, please can I say something now? I think it must be my turn."

> Oi! Cut it out!

Q3 – *You haven't seen someone for a week as it's been school holidays. How do you both get to tell each other all your news?*

a) Just start talking and keep going. It's fascinating stuff.

b) Sigh loudly and look bored while they talk, to make them hurry up.

c) Try as hard as you can to take turns, so the conversation flows.

The best answers to choose if you want to be a good friend are the c) ones. Yep, important as your thoughts and feelings are, a *friend* needs to remember that other people have them too.

47

How to begin

There are all kinds of ways of meeting and making a new friend, but the scenario on this page and the next shows you how to begin getting to know someone in a gradual, gentle way by being friendly, asking questions, listening and being kind. It's an approach that usually works.

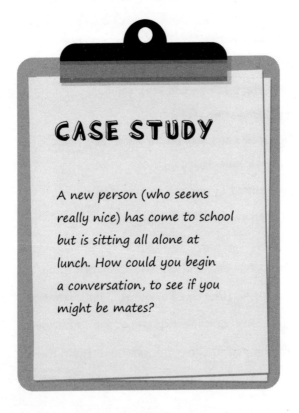

CASE STUDY

A new person (who seems really nice) has come to school but is sitting all alone at lunch. How could you begin a conversation, to see if you might be mates?

START HERE

Hi.

1 Smile, say 'hi', and tell them your name, then ask what theirs is. If they smile, or turn to face you, all good.

2 Say something nice if you can. That always makes people feel good.

Fab trainers.

3 If they respond in a friendly way, you could ask them another question, such as how long they have been at the school.

4 You could ask if they're settling in OK. Is there anything they need to know, or are not sure about?

5 By asking questions, try to find something you both like. How about a new comedy series that's just started?

6 If things are still going well, ask if they fancy doing something together, like going for bubble tea in town.

7 If they say 'yes', suggest some dates.* Now's the time to talk about yourself, and answer their questions.

8 A tiny seed of a new friendship has been sown. You've done the hardest part. Now, it's over to you two.

*If it's a 'no', don't panic. See pages 50 and 51 for some advice.

FRIENDSHIP

49

Expect the best

Awkward.

That scenario went well, but sometimes, however much you want to be someone's friend, they don't feel the same. It happens, and it's tough. It can help if you recognize the signs before you get to the rejection part, and know how to respond, but try not to take it to heart if it doesn't work out. It's a good idea to expect the best of people you meet, but sometimes they can, and will, disappoint you. 'Reading' other people is tricky, and takes practice – well, it takes a lifetime, really.

There's lots more about how to cope with friendships that go wrong in Chapters 5 and 9, but you may get a few knock-backs. After all, everyone can't like EVERYONE, can they?

Here are some 'Friendship Red Flags' to look out for:

 If the person you're talking to isn't listening, looks at their phone, or scans the room, it's time to move on.

 If someone rolls their eyes, makes a bored face or doesn't answer you... well, first and foremost, that's very rude. Leave them to it.

 If you message someone to arrange to meet up and they don't respond, try again. If they blank you again, you deserve better.

 If a person ignores you, or says something unkind, walk away. Being unkind is a no-go: kindness is the keystone of friendship.

THE
MAKING FRIENDS
QUIZ

Now that you've read this chapter all about how to make a friend, it's time to test out your new skills. There are no 'right' answers, but some are MUCH better than others.

Choose just **one** answer for each question:

Q1 – What should you do FIRST if you meet a new person you like, and want to get to know?

a) Bounce up to them and hug them. Everyone loves a hug, right?

b) Smile, introduce yourself and ask them their name.

c) Tell them you have EXACTLY the same bag/phone/shoes as they do.

d) Ask them lots of questions about themselves.

Q2 – If you're shy about talking to someone new, which of these things might help you?

a) Avoid them. If they want to talk to you, they'll find you.

b) Remind yourself that they might be a bit shy, too. You might really get on.

c) Take some deep, slow breaths to calm yourself down a little.

d) Write them a note. It's much less exposing.

Q3 – The new girl didn't come and sit in the empty chair next to you, but sat on her own instead. What do you do?

a) Decide not to bother with her. Life's too short.

b) Smile at her, but respect her choice.

c) Go and sit next to her and tell her all about your new dog.

d) Wave at her across the room so that she notices you.

The most sensitive answers are the b) ones, and the least kind, the a) ones. The others are in-between!

CHAPTER FOUR

How friendships grow

Friendships can begin in a few moments, or with a few words, but it takes time for them to grow stronger and deeper.

This chapter is full of suggestions for how to nurture your friendships and be the best friend you can be. Being a good friend is one of the most important jobs you'll ever have, so it's worth knowing a bit more about how to do it well, isn't it?

My mission — to be a SUPER friend!

SWOOSH

Understanding

There are lots of ways friendships can grow, but at the heart of a good, equal friendship is something called **empathy**. Here's a definition of what it means:

empathy

**the ability to understand
and share the feelings
of another person**

Showing a friend that you can 'share their feelings' – feel sad when they are sad, and happy when they are feeling good – is a key ingredient in the friendship mix. And you need empathy *from* your friends, too:

it's a two-way thing.

Patience

When you first find a person you really click with, it's a wonderful feeling. You may want to chat, text, message or call them all the time. Without wanting to sound negative, it's sometimes worth being patient, and taking your time.

It can be tricky to hit the sweet spot between letting someone know you like them and overwhelming them (which can make people panic a bit). If a new friendship is getting a bit intense, give it some room to breathe: like a plant, it needs time and space to flourish.

Give me some space, please!

Did you see that film?

Do you like this game?

Where shall we go on Saturday?

Taking turns

Sometimes, all you want to do when you meet friends is TALK! You might feel as if you just can't say everything you want to say fast enough. This is understandable, and it's great to talk to friends, but it's also important to listen to them.

Remember how it feels when someone talks AT you for ages, and you can't get a word in? Or when another person doesn't seem to hear what you say, as they are so desperate for more airtime? It's not good, and you soon get fed up, don't you?

The best tip for avoiding this is to *make a real point of taking turns* – it's as simple as that. This may feel a bit weird at first, but it gets easier. Then, you'll be able to be a little more flexible because everyone will feel heard.

Listening is key to a balanced friendship, and shows real empathy, so:

aim to be a great listener.

Don't expect perfection

Most friendships have a few rough patches: they are part of how human relationships work. (You'll find out how to manage bigger friendship problems in Chapter 9.) There are a few things it's really worth keeping in mind when you're with your mates. Turn the page to find a list of them, a 'blueprint' for friendship, in a way, but remember, it's those shared 'core values' that matter most.

FRIENDSHIP BLUEPRINT

- Always be kind. Everyone has their 'off' days and bad moods, so if your friends do, try to be understanding. Then, you can hope for the same from them.

Burger?

Pizza?

- Be willing to meet friends halfway if you can't agree on something. It's not showing weakness, but real strength of character.

OK, burger this week, pizza next!

- Nobody else is inside your head, so if a good friend lets you down, give them another chance. If they do it again and again, however, they are not good friend material.*

- Respect their views, decisions and wishes, as they are just as valid as yours. Friendship includes the chance to learn about someone else, and see what matters to them. It can be a steep learning curve!

*See Chapter 10 for more.

Be there

So far, you've had a few pointers for keeping your friendships on track, all of which centre on **respect** and **kindness**. But there's one more thing to mention before we move on. You may remember from page 29 that the three key qualities in a good friendship are:

Respect • Kindness • Loyalty

Loyalty can be summed up in these four words:

'being there for someone'.

All the other factors in your friendship boil down to this, really. For your friendships to thrive, you may need to defend each other and offer support if and when it's needed. This is what 'being there' really means. It may not always be easy, but it will usually be worth it.

THE KINDNESS QUIZ?

Right, time to go back to kindness, which is so vital in friendship. Which do you think is the **kindest** answer to these questions?

Choose **one** answer for each question:

Q1 – You get on well with someone in another class, but it's difficult to find time to meet up. A band you both like is playing a gig on Saturday. **DO YOU:**

a) Buy them a ticket and tell them you've done so. They can't refuse to come with you then, can they?

b) Tell them you're going and that you'd love it if they joined you, but no pressure.

c) Go on your own, and if you see them there, stay cool, perhaps say 'hi' but enjoy the music anyway.

The FLYING BIRDS
ADMIT ONE
The FLYING BIRDS
28th May
7.00PM
ROW E SEAT 17

Q2 – A friend has just come back from an amazing holiday and wants to tell you all about it after school, but you have piles of homework. **DO YOU:**

a) Tell them you're really busy, so you won't have time, but you're glad they enjoyed the trip.

b) Explain that you've got stuff to do, but that it would be great to chat about it for a while.

c) Forget your homework and say you'd love to hear all about it and see every single photo.

Q3 – You really want to watch the new movie of your favourite musical this weekend, but your friend prefers action movies. **DO YOU:**

a) Refuse to give in. Tell them that if you have to sit through one more action movie, you'll lose the plot.

b) Let them win and wait to see the musical, but say that next time, it's your turn to choose.

c) Say that you are going to watch it with someone else because you're so fed up with their attitude.

You've probably realized that the b) answers are the kindest, most patient, most empathetic options to choose.

CHAPTER FIVE

Best friends: good, bad or both?

You'll meet a lot of different people during your lifetime – thousands, probably. You'll probably make a lot of friends, too. Whether you'll have a best friend, a 'bestie', is less certain. Many people never do – they have lots of friends instead. You can read about friendship groups in Chapter 6, but this part of the book looks at **best** friends.

I love spending time with you!

Having just one person who completely 'gets' you can be amazing: you're soulmates, you finish each other's sentences and like all the same stuff.

This is all great, but unfortunately this very closeness can cause a few problems, especially if things go wrong.

Good and not-so-good

So, what are the **good** things about having one really close friend? Well, here are some of them:

- You feel secure and needed, knowing that they will always have your back.
- It's reassuring to be with someone who thinks the same as you and shares your core values.
- It's easier to share secrets, or talk about difficult stuff, with one person, rather than a group.
- You don't have to try as hard with others if you've always got your bestie close by.

Sounds good, doesn't it? And it can be...

...but here are some of the possibly **not-so-good** things about best friends too:

- You may not get to know any other people and both become isolated.
- If your best mate is ill, or away, you could have a lonely time.
- If tension builds up between you, you may quarrel to release it and things will be stressful.
- You may both start to feel shy, or find it difficult to socialize with anyone else.

Being aware of these drawbacks will help you to avoid them as you meet people and form friendships. As a general rule, besties are wonderful things, but it's a good idea to make sure you DO talk to other people as well, just in case.

I think I WILL meet up with Belle. She keeps asking...

Being equal

If you have a best friend, it's really important to feel you are both **equal** partners in the friendship. Sadly, if one person is more powerful, the other one can feel forced to do or accept things they don't want to, for fear of losing their friend.

Take a look at this tricky scenario to see how easily this can happen:

Sam and Lily have been best friends for the whole of the school year, but now, Lily wants to go to a party where they both know people might be drinking a lot. Lily promises she won't drink, but Sam is unsure. Lily says Sam is boring, and that she won't be Sam's bestie if she won't go to the party with her.

WHAT DO YOU THINK SAM SHOULD DO?

a) Go with her. Lily is her best friend after all.

b) Refuse to go and risk their friendship ending.

c) Explain how strongly she feels and hope Lily understands.

Can you help me choose?

Sam

Have you ever been in a situation a bit like this? Again, there is no 'right' answer, but you can probably see that c) is the best choice. Sam must be true to herself, and if Lily can't see and respect that, perhaps their friendship is not an equal one.

When things go wrong

Sometimes, we make a friend that stays
a friend for life, but this is pretty rare.
Most of the problems with having
a best friend tend to
happen when the
friendship ends.

Sorry, but I don't think this is working any more.

Oh, right.

This can happen for different reasons, and
many of them are natural, and even for the
best. You may have had a niggling feeling
that something was wrong, feel uncomfortable
talking to your friend, or notice that they are
not replying to messages. Sadly, it happens.

Here are some of the main reasons why close friendships can fall apart:

- **The friends have such a big quarrel that they can't find a way to make up.**

- **People change: a friendship may change too, and not work well any more.**

- **One friend might find a new best mate, or start a new relationship and drop you.**

- **One friend moves away, leaving the other on their own.**

I promise I'll keep in touch.

What next?

If this happens to you, whether you feel like the 'dropped', or the 'dropper', it can be devastating. All those cosy feelings to do with having one close friend are gone, and instead, you just feel *lonely*. It's really tough, but – harsh as it may sound – this is all part of that rollercoaster ride called life. You WILL get over it and make new friends in time.

I'm not sure what to do next. Kel always knew.

There's lots more about getting hurt by friends in Chapter 9.

For now, here are some ways of coping with the end of a friendship and starting to move on:

Think back over how things were before the friendship ended. Were there a few problems? Might you both be better off this way?

Make sure you hang out with other people. (If you always did, this will be easier, but if you didn't, be honest now. They'll know what's happened to you.)

Be open to new things, new people — ones you may not have considered before. This could be the start of something good.

Say 'yes', not 'no'!

YOUR 'BESTIES' QUIZ

Now that you've read all about the good and not-so-good sides of having just one best friend, choose what you feel is the **best answer** to these three questions:

Q1 – Your best friend has started not replying to your messages and avoiding you in class.
DO YOU:

a) Avoid them right back. Two can play at that game.

b) Ask them straight what's going on. You're really angry.

c) Tell them you are hurt, but give them some space.

> Hello Drew. Missed you at the game. OK?

> Hi mate. Not seen you around. R U ill?

> Everything alright? Did I do something wrong?

> ...

Q2 – You really REALLY want to go on a school trip, but your best friend is a bit worried about the cost. **DO YOU:**

a) Explain how you feel and go. It's your life after all.
b) Miss the trip to support your mate. End of.
c) See if you can find a solution together, so that they can come.

Q3 – Your best friend is moving away next term. You are very worried about being alone when they do. **DO YOU:**

a) Drop them straight away: you need to look after Number One.
b) Start seeing much less of them, so you get used to it.
c) Start expanding your network of friends, but still see your bestie.

As usual, there are no 'right' answers. You need to choose which one you feel will work best for you. If you chose the c) answers, yay! It sounds like you have a good idea of how to keep a friendship balanced.

CHAPTER SIX

Groups, gangs, cliques and tribes

Being part of a group of friends can be the best thing in the world. You hang out together, do stuff you all enjoy and really feel you're **safe**. And you can use great, feel-good words like 'us' and 'we'. Awwww. It's more serious warm fuzziness, basically.

Aww, you guys.

Sounds good, and it really can be, but people are complicated, so any group of them is going to be a mix of a lot of different personalities. This chapter looks at how groups work, and how to ride the waves of all those egos and stay true to yourself.

How to join a group

Actually, perhaps you aren't part of a friendship group yet, but want to be? Well, some experts have compared joining a group of people to joining the traffic on a busy road. Put simply, you need to join without annoying anyone or forcing them to brake! It's sometimes called the 'watch and blend' approach.

Here are some pointers that might help you join a group:

1 Watch what's going on. Does everyone seem friendly? (The expressions on their faces might tell you.)

HA HA HA

HA HA HA

HA HA

2 What do they chat about? Is it something you could contribute to, or know about? Do you feel you would fit in with them?

3 Remembering that traffic image, go closer. Try saying something that ties into their conversation, like 'I love that movie too — gotta love a zombie!' or 'I can't get above the third level — any clues?'.

4 Now it's time to try to blend into the chat, but wait until it feels right. You don't need to be pushy, or say a lot. That can be annoying.

5 If the group talks about doing something fun together, and you feel confident, try asking if you can tag along. Hopefully, they'll agree*.

*If they don't, it happens. You could try again, or perhaps they're just not the right group for you. You'll find your tribe if you know what to look for.

Who's who?

So, you're in... Now what?

Well, you'll probably start to notice that the people in groups behave differently. Researchers have looked at the roles friends tend to play in groups, and found things sometimes work differently for boys and girls. These roles can seem like stereotypes, but nobody matches them exactly: every person, in every group, is slightly different. They are a rough overview. You may feel that you don't fit into any of these roles and that's fine: people are pretty complex!

Whether you recognize these roles or not, knowing a little more about them may help you understand what's going on in your friendship group, and help you decide what role you would like to play in it, if you want to.

Being tough

In some groups, the main aim of everyone involved is to *avoid looking wimpy*. This means that things often get very physical, or are about being 'hard' or 'cool'. This is more often the case with boys, but by no means always.

Here are some of these 'tough' roles:

THE RINGLEADER

This is the boss, the person everyone looks to for decisions and for approval. They might set tricky, physical challenges that others have to do if they want to stay in the group and not be seen as 'weedy' or 'bottling it'.

THE DEPUTY

...or Sidekick — the Ringleader's right-hand person. They might see their role as making sure everyone stays in line and does what the Ringleader expects. They will also try to make sure they stay safely indispensable.

THE JOKER

Many groups have a member whose role is to make the others laugh, to play up and take away some of the tension in being tough. A Joker can feel trapped, fed up with never being taken seriously, though.

The dreaded FOMO*

In other friendship groups, things may operate differently. The fear of being excluded, or left out, is very powerful. The need to belong and to be accepted is strong, which can lead to gossip, rivalry and lots of emotional fallout.

Here are some typical roles in this kind of group, but, again, there's no 'one size fits all':

THE BANKER

This role involves getting friends' trust and then 'banking' their secrets until they can be used for the Banker's own gain. Nobody dares cross the Banker, because they know too much... Bad news.

I won't tell ANYONE.

*'FOMO' = **F**ear **o**f **M**issing **O**ut.

THE MESSENGER

This person may spend a lot of time talking to and about other people. Their role is to pass gossip, rumour or criticism between everyone (and stay safely OUT of quarrels).

THE PLEASER

This role is one that's easy to spot. A Pleaser doesn't disagree with anyone (even when they actually do). Their aim is to keep their head low and avoid confrontation at all costs. Exhausting.

Wait — there's more

There are two roles that we haven't looked at yet. They may be played slightly differently, as people don't fit any stereotype completely, but you'll probably recognize both of them.

THE CONSCIENCE

Often, there is someone in a group whose role is to tell the others when they have gone too far, or are out of order.

Wait!

This role can be super-stressful. There's more about the pressures involved on pages 100–102.

THE LOSER

...or Scapegoat, or Outsider. This person gets blamed when things go wrong, teased, left out and given unpopular tasks or 'dares' to do. It's sad, but true.

Including the Outsider

Gangs, groups and cliques are a vital part of many young peoples' lives. Belonging to one can make a huge difference to your wellbeing, and even your mental health. But what about the people who are always left out?

When we defined 'empathy', it focused on the importance of trying to understand, and share, another person's feelings. If there's an outsider in your group, how do you imagine they must feel?

Maybe YOU can be the one who tries to include that person, and makes sure they're OK? If you can empathize with someone who's on the outside, you'll know to treat them as you hope people would treat you – with kindness. Who knows?

One day, it could be **YOU**.

If you feel left out of a group yourself, you'll know how hard it is, but remember, if the foundations of friendship are kindness, honesty and loyalty, perhaps it's time to make new, better friends?

So, who do you play?

Do you play any of these roles in your group? If you do, are you happy about it? If you're not in a group at the moment, no problem. Everything you're reading in this book will help you make good friendship choices. There's a lot in a 'great mate' toolkit, but don't worry, you'll get there.

THE FRIENDSHIP ROLES QUIZ

Let's see how many roles you recognize in the possible answers to these questions, now you know more about them. Then, choose what you think you would do in each situation:

Q1 – Your group wants to go to the beach at the weekend, but you find swimming in the sea a bit scary. **DO YOU:**

a) Go anyway. You have to, or it's FOMO Central.

b) Refuse to go and insist the group doesn't either.

c) Say you'll go, but explain why you won't be swimming.

Q2 – One person in your group is having a hard time at home. The others are fed up with all the moaning and want to drop them. **DO YOU:**

a) Go with whatever the others decide. It's safer.

b) Firmly tell that person to stop moaning: it's getting you down.

c) Be the better friend. Listen, and say you're always there if they need someone to talk to.

Q3 – A member of your group has been shoplifting. They say it's easy and 'nobody ever gets caught'. They want the whole group to do it next weekend. **DO YOU:**

a) Keep quiet and agree to go, whatever you really think.

b) Tell them not to be so stupid and that you're going to tell.

c) Say, clearly, that you aren't doing it, and think it's wrong.

Turn the page to see what your answers reveal.

Sometimes it's really hard to make the 'right' choice when you're with a group, but if you chose the c) answers, well done. They best reflect the most important things in friendship:

Respect   **Kindness**

Loyalty

... and **Honesty**, which isn't always easy.

There's more about coping with pressures in a group in the next chapter, but if you chose those answers, you're already playing the most important role of all:

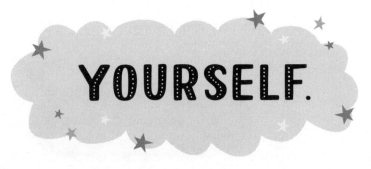

YOURSELF.

CHAPTER SEVEN

Out in the cold

We touched on some of the pressures that you might feel in a group of friends in Chapter 6. The pressure to fit in and do what everyone else is doing because it's the most *comfortable* option (even if you don't feel it's the *right* one) is probably the biggest one of all: it's called **peer pressure**.

Relax, it's just a selfie, Lois!

In this part of the book, we'll take a closer look at some of the ways peer pressure can affect you, and suggest some ways of coping with it.

Peer pressure

Your *peers* are people who are roughly the same age as you and at a similar stage in their lives – in school, forming friendships and relationships, discovering what kind of person they want to be.

None of your peers is just like you, however. It can be easy to think there's a checklist for being someone at your stage of life, a list of things you must have, must do and must believe, but this really isn't the case:

What you need to be a happy young person:

- ✗ no flaws whatsoever
- ✗ hundreds of friends and followers
- ? all the best gear
- ✗ top grades in school
- ✗ be brilliant at all sports
- ☹ be adored by everyone, all the time

This isn't me at all.

Did that list sound achievable? Nope, of course not. Life isn't like this!

Every single one of us is *wonderfully* **different** and we all need to find happiness in our own way.

Being different is a GOOD thing, but pressure from your peers to fit into a standard 'mould' can sometimes make it difficult for you to make your own decisions and choices. Everyone wants to be liked and included: it's only natural, and it feels safe... but it's not always **right**.

I'm not the same as the others.

Don't worry. It's OK just to be YOU!

There may be times when you feel you disagree with your peers, and want to behave differently, but it's tricky to go against the crowd.

How would you react?

To see how peer pressure works, look at these typical examples:

MEAN MATES

There's a new boy in your class and he's not fitting in well. He's a bit different, shy and wears very 'out there' clothes. You think he seems interesting, but everyone in your group is teasing him and he looks so unhappy. **WHAT DO YOU DO?**

a) Stay out of it. He has to fight his own battles.

b) Suggest that your friends leave him alone, because it's unkind.

c) Do what everyone's doing. You need to fit in too, after all.

This is a tricky one, isn't it? The new boy isn't a mate, but being unkind is nasty. Would you be brave enough to say so? If you think you would be, you'll have chosen b). OK, next one...

FOMO (**F**ear **o**f **M**issing **O**ut) is very real, but keeping your word is important, too. If you feel that should be your priority on Saturday afternoon, you'll have chosen c).

What about this scenario?

BOSSY BOOTS

The (very bossy) leader of your group says you all need to wear the same type of boots to show unity and loyalty to each other. You hate those boots, don't find them comfortable AND they are very expensive. **WHAT DO YOU DO?**

a) Tell the group it's a no-go for you, and why.

b) Pester your parents or carers to buy the boots for you. It has to happen.

c) Search for a second-hand pair, and put up with the pain.

You MUST have us!

Strong characters need to be challenged, but could you tell this leader that you're not going to do as they say? It might make you very unpopular and see you left out. If you think you are up to it, you'll have chosen a).

We'll always be your go-to.

Reality check

But let's get real here. Choosing the 'brave' option in those three questions is a whole lot easier than it would be in reality. For a start, your group might not appreciate your honesty, and feel threatened by it, and you. You might also make them feel bad about their own behaviour. No, it's not easy at all.

The pressure to go along with what everyone else is doing, wearing, liking, following or saying is MASSIVE, so never underestimate it.

Some experts talk about something called 'groupthink', which means that everyone in a group follows a powerful personality even when they **know** they're making bad choices. Going against the crowd risks you being left 'out in the cold'. Bad news.

So how do you stay true to you, and survive peer pressure? Well, there are tactics to try, but none of them is easy: each demands some real, old-fashioned courage, in fact.

Here are some of your options:

- Express your views clearly and calmly (and don't start with 'I'm sorry, but...'). If you need to, keep repeating your opinion until you're sure people hear you.

- Decide to be a free agent, or a floater, moving between friendship groups rather than committing to just one. Then, you're always free to make your own decisions.

I'm the master of my own destiny!

- Suggest an alternative to any ideas or choices you disagree with. Sometimes, finding a 'goal' for the group, like raising funds for charity, can help heal divisions and unite you all.

- Keep reminding yourself that you don't HAVE to be in the gang, or group, at all. Might life be a lot easier with a few good friends, instead of always striving to fit in with a whole group?

This way to a better future.

EXIT

101

- If you aren't happy with anything your group is doing, but they won't stop, gradually begin to move away from them, and start to spend your time with people you do like.

- If you're feeling a lot of pressure to do something you don't want to, talk to someone you trust. It takes courage to stand up to the crowd, so ask for support if you need it.

Finally, remember that being

kind, honest, loyal
and **showing others respect**

is VITAL to friendship. If you believe that but your group doesn't, you might need to leave it and face being out in the cold until you find some real friends. Because you will.

CHAPTER EIGHT

Social media

Is your phone often the last thing you look at each day, and the first thing you reach for each morning? Do you get a bit twitchy if you haven't checked your notifications lately?

Today, social media is a big part of everyday life, especially for young people. It connects you to the world beyond home and school and offers endless entertainment and information, plus a running commentary on what others online are doing/ feeling/eating/watching/playing/wearing/thinking or believing. Is it a good thing? Well, yes... and no.

This chapter looks at both what social media can add to your life and to your friendships, and what it can take away.

What's it all about?

So, it's a part of all our lives, but what does 'social media' really **mean**? Put very simply, it means communicating with other people online rather than in person, face-to-face.

There are lots of different ways of doing this, and LOTS of apps, forums, chats, networks, groups and platforms. All of them work in slightly different ways, but they all aim to put people in touch with other people. Sound good? Well, they can be.

Let's start with the many **good** things about social media...

This is going to be such a great pic for my social media feed!

It helps people to stay in touch.

It's great for chatting in groups, not just to one person.

It's ideal for notifying a lot of people about something important, FAST.

You can ask for help, and get answers from lots of other people.

You can play with other gamers, which can be more fun than playing alone.

You can find out what's going on in your local area.

You may get a happy 'buzz' when people interact with you online.

You can learn about the world, and what's going on in it, 24/7.

You might prefer to get to know people online, before meeting them in person.

Sadly, there are some **not-so-good** things about social media, too. Here are the main ones:

If you put something on social media, it may not be possible to delete it – ever.

It can gobble up your time, as it's easy to browse and scroll for AGES.

People can say unkind, cruel things they would not say in person.*

You might see something you wish you hadn't, but can't 'unsee'.

People can ignore, ghost, block or have a 'beef' (argument) with you.

It can be addictive. Yes, really. Let's find out more about that one...

*You'll find more about unkind friends (or 'frenemies'), and bullying and trolling, in Chapters 10 and 11 of this book.

Give me likes!

As you've already found out, it's completely natural to want to fit in and be accepted, and we need to feel this in our online life as much as we do in our face-to-face one. So, we rely on our online friends to give us that approval and feeling of belonging by seeking what is called **validation** from them – which often means *likes*. Not getting them can really affect your mood.

My last selfie got 247 likes, but this one has only got 135. I'm so depressed.

Whenever someone asks to be your 'friend', or 'likes' or shares your post or picture, your brain releases a shot of hormones called **endorphins**. This can make you feel good and give you some of that 'warm fuzziness' again, which is great.

For some people, however, the more of this feel-good stuff they have, the more they want, and this is where the risk of addiction lurks. Social media friends can make you feel good, but on the flip side, if people *don't* like or share your stuff, or, even worse, say unkind things about it, it's very easy to get really down.

Also, there's no shutting your bedroom door and getting away from it if you want to: social media is there, all the time, just waiting for you to log on.

So what do I DO?

It's great to feel part of a big online community, but if you find yourself having to work really hard to *stay* a part of it – always feeling you should be posting, checking, hoping and waiting for likes or comments – well, that's soooooo exhausting. You might feel tired in school, find it hard to focus on your work, and may well begin to wonder if the 'friends' out there are really friends at all.

If this is you, you are not alone, but it could be that social media is becoming a bit of a problem, and you need to take a break from it. You need to **control it, rather than let it control you,** because being true to yourself is just as important in this part of your life as in any other part.

Keeping things in check

Here are some simple tips for keeping social media in check. Try them, or some of them, and see how you feel. It could be that you need to take a break.

- Try not to keep your phone in the room you sleep in. Research shows it can stop you relaxing and going to sleep.

- Don't reply to everything straight away. Take a breath, count to ten and then decide if you really need to.

- If you find it hard to log off, try handing your phone to someone else and ask them to do it for you for the first few times.

- Try not to comment on gossip or squabbles. You may regret it. It's better to sort things face-to-face.

- How about keeping family meal times a 'phone-free zone'? If that's when you all meet up, it's the only time you can chat.

Hmm, maybe it IS time to take a break...

- Remember, online friends can't give you a hug, if that's what you need (and we all do, sometimes). A hug emoji just isn't the same, is it?

THE SOCIAL MEDIA QUIZ

So, you've read the theory, and looked at the good and bad sides of social media. Now it's time to think about the part it plays in your life, and whether you've got the balance right yet.

Q1 – It's really late, but your mates are chatting online about a movie you didn't enjoy much. **DO YOU:**

a) Say you need to sleep and leave the chat.
b) Doze off, but wake up every so often to add a few meaningful words.
c) Stay awake. You cannot risk missing out on anything. Ever.

Q2 – You put a new selfie up this afternoon, but hardly anyone has liked it yet. **DO YOU:**

a) Give it time. Everyone's probably busy, or not seen it.
b) Edit it. Perhaps you could look even better.

c)   Take it down. Your mates obviously
     hate it, and you.

Q3 – *Your mate has sent you a meme that you
find a bit offensive.* **DO YOU:**

a)   Delete it and DM your friend to tell
     them what you felt.
b)   Like it. It's only a meme.
c)   Comment, saying what you thought.
     Your mate needs to know.

Q4 – *You realize on the way to school that you've
left your phone at home. Your dad's working from
home today.* **DO YOU:**

a)   Resign yourself to not being online
     until after school.
b)   Call Dad from a mate's phone and
     ask him to bring it into school asap.
c)   Decide to risk being late for school
     and go back to fetch it.

Turn the page to see what
your answers reveal.

If you chose c) answers, staying in the loop is pretty vital to you. Perhaps it's time to pull back a little, and do more other stuff instead.

If you chose a), well done. You seem to have social media in perspective, and have the balance between your face-to-face and your online life about right.

Hmm, you b)-choosers. Perhaps it's time to have a look at your relationship with all things online. Life is out there, remember.

Time for balance

If this chapter has made you think about the role social media plays in your life, that's good, but it's worth remembering that online friends can really give you a sense of belonging and acceptance, even if you have never met them.

Real connections can be formed online. In fact, you may feel that you have found your tribe there and feel more able to be yourself online than anywhere else: a lot of people do. But you may need more...

If this is you, it's a good idea to try to meet up with 'live' friends too, if only because it means you get away from a screen for a while. Taking a break from social media – going for a walk with the dog, having a (phone) chat with a mate, making a snack – all these simple things refresh you in more ways than one. Finally, just make sure you remember to spend some time living your *real* life as well as your online one. A balance is best.

CHAPTER NINE

Falling out... and making up

You will almost certainly fall out with your friends at times, even your best ones. It's not great, but whether it's a minor beef or a full-blown meltdown, it need not mean the end of your friendship. In fact, it may even make it stronger.

> I know things are not going well, but I'm sure we can fix it.

This chapter will help you steer your way through these tricky times and show you some tactics for surviving friendship fall-outs (and, hopefully, staying friends). You might need to take some new ideas on board, but they are all part of the friendship checklist.

Tough love

Put simply, the main thing you need to get you through the ups and downs of your friendships is something called **resilience**. In a dictionary, you'll see it defined something like this:

resilience

the ability to recover from difficulties; toughness

If you have this 'toughness', you believe that you *can* and *will* get through difficult times. You'll also try not to let those times spoil your life until the happy day you emerge from them and life is better again. Yay! This may sound easy, but it takes practice, like any other new skill.

Having resilience doesn't mean becoming hard, or nasty – nobody wants that. It's more about seeing things in perspective and protecting yourself from emotional pain. We humans are sensitive creatures, easily hurt, and the people close to us can hurt us more than anyone.

Think of resilience as an invisible shell around you, if you like: something that keeps you feeling OK when things are going wrong. Research shows that it can help you survive and recover from the ups and downs in relationships. Sound good? It is.

But before you find out how to develop some of it, we need to look at chimps.

Did someone say chimps?

It's only natural

Falling out with those close to you is actually pretty natural. Animals growl, peck, claw or scratch each other, and things can get pretty vicious, but once it's all over, many of them say "I'm sorry" (according to animal experts). Some species do this by licking each other, some snooze in a big pile, and chimpanzees, for example, pick out and eat each other's fleas. Yum.

It's worth remembering that, if you spend a lot of time with someone, there may well be times when you don't agree, really annoy each other, or even want never, EVER to see them again, but you can usually find a way to say sorry, and be even better mates. (You don't actually have to eat any fleas...)

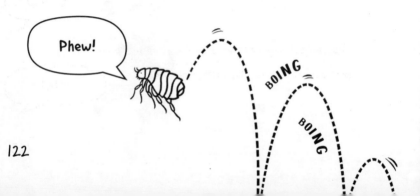

Phew!

BOING

BOING

What we fall out about

OK, let's look at some of the many, many things friends might fall out about. Are any of them familiar?

Your mate broke your brand new swimming goggles and can't afford to replace them.

DEVASTATED

You told your friend that you don't like someone and they told them.

FURIOUS

A friend wants to copy your notes again (because they NEVER listen in class).

ANNOYED

You showed your bestie the outfit you're going to wear to a party and they've copied it.

STUNNED

Your mate organizes weekly football matches, but you're not in the team this week.

HURT

The list of scenarios could go on and on. If nothing like any of them has ever happened to you, you're **very lucky indeed**. If it has, you are not alone. (In fact, we'll come back to some of them later, so watch this space...)

Resilience tactics

So, you've fallen out with a friend. It's early days, it hurts, and you're thinking about what they said/didn't say/did or didn't do all the time. You could really do with some of that toughness to help you until things are sorted out, couldn't you? Here are a few resilience-building tactics to try:

- **SHUT IT DOWN**
  Is going over and over what's happened helping you? No? OK, then it's time to try to switch those thoughts off. Do something you LIKE, that will make you feel GOOD. What you do is up to you!

You could:

- Sing your favourite song **VERY LOUDLY.**
- Make pancakes.
- Call your granny.
- Go for a power walk.
- Eat buttered toast.

• BE KIND TO YOURSELF

Whatever happened, happened, but it takes time for the dust to settle after a big argument. If this isn't the first time you've fallen out with your friend, did anything make you feel better last time? Yes? Well, do that thing again immediately!

• TAKE STOCK

Look back over your friendship. Has this happened before? Do you think you can get past this quarrel too, in time? If not, perhaps you need to take stock, and consider your needs a bit more.

• TAKE A BREATH

Before you fire off bitter texts or unfriend the Universe, think twice. Will it solve things, or could it make them worse? Take a few long, slow, deep breaths. Life will go on and your hurt will heal, whether you make up or not. Really.

I feel a bit calmer already, out in the fresh air.

Making up

There are many different ways of making up with a friend after you've fallen out: you need to find the one that works best for both of you. Some of them are very straightforward (and may or may not make things better). Others need a little more thought and a lot more maturity (but are more likely to repair the friendship long-term). See what you think.

Simple tactics:

* Hug your mate so hard that they HAVE to laugh.
* Just pretend the argument hasn't happened.
* Buy your friend a small gift or treat.
* Suggest a fun outing together for next weekend.

Some fall-outs are more difficult to fix. Turn the page to find some tips for sorting things out.

Trickier tactics:

* Compromise:

This means accepting that both of you are partly responsible for what happened. Talking it through and meeting somewhere in the middle blame-wise shows that you both really value the friendship.

Sounds fair. Let's shake on it.

* Agreeing to disagree:

This means facing the fact that you are never going to see this problem the same way, but choosing to stay mates anyway. Decide to draw a line under it, put it to bed, move on (and lots of other daft clichés).

* Being the bigger person:

Choosing this option might mean you have to let something go that you feel was wrong, or that upset you. It isn't easy, but sometimes it's best. You need to decide if you'd rather be totally right, or keep your friendship.

* Saying sorry:

If you think you've upset a friend, or behaved badly, it's important to accept responsibility, and say sorry. This usually reduces tension, and may even strengthen your friendship. You might find it makes you feel better about yourself, too. Say sorry, and mean it.

THE FRIENDSHIP FIXING QUIZ

Remember those 'reasons for falling out' on page 123? Now that you've read more about them, let's see which solution for these situations you would choose now.

Q1 – Your mate broke your brand new swimming goggles and can't afford to replace them. **DO YOU:**

a) Tell them you need new ones. End of.

b) Say you know it was an accident and let it go.

c) Replace the goggles yourself, but ask your friend to pay you back in instalments.

Q2 – You told your friend that you don't like someone and they've told them. **DO YOU:**

a) Drop them immediately. They've crossed a line.

b) Hide how you really feel and tell them it doesn't matter.

c) Explain that you feel let down and believe you deserve an apology.

Q3 – A friend wants to copy your notes again (because they NEVER listen in class). **DO YOU:**

a) Tell them you've had enough and threaten to tell the teacher.

b) Give them the notes. It's not worth falling out about.

c) Say OK, but this is the very last time, and mean it.

Q4 – Your bestie has bought exactly the same outfit as yours for a party. Sooo embarrassing! **DO YOU:**

a) Insist they return it and get another outfit TODAY.

b) Laugh about it. These things happen. It might even be funny!

c) Say it seems fairer for them to wear something else.

Turn the page to see what your answers reveal.

So, the most understanding answers to these problems, the ones that are most likely to see you having balanced, lasting friendships, are the c) ones. They allow you to be honest and say how you feel, but move past the problem. We ALL make mistakes. Most friendships are pretty flexible, and will survive a few ups and downs.

It's worth reminding yourself again of those core friendship values:

respect, kindness and **loyalty**.

Perhaps we should add **patience** too, when it comes to fallings-out.

And finally, if you chose the a) answers folks, imagine it was YOU who had made those mistakes. How would you want **your** mates to react?

CHAPTER TEN

Frenemies, fake and toxic friends

We looked at what makes a *good* friend, and how to be one, in Chapter 2. This part of the book will help you identify a *not-so-good* one. Sadly, not everyone is kind; at some point, you will probably come across people who are very *unkind*. Luckily, knowing how to spot them will help.

You may have heard the words 'frenemies', or 'toxic', or 'fake' friends. These are all ways of describing people that can be very **good** at making you feel very **bad**. Even worse, they can be experts at *hiding* their nastiness from other people, so their victims feel misunderstood and isolated. What can you do about them? Well, this chapter offers tactics for kicking frenemies out of your life – and keeping them out.

The good stuff

So, after everything you've read so far, what qualities do you now think make a good friend? See if you can come up with a personal checklist. Here are some things that might be on it, but your list should be all *yours*:

A good friend is someone who:

* You enjoy being with.

* Is loyal, and always has your back.

> Mate, I didn't do it.

> Don't worry, I saw it all. I'll tell them it wasn't you.

* Has time for you, and listens to what you think and feel.

* Lets you relax and be yourself. Yay!

* Doesn't make you do things you don't want to.

* Makes you feel good and full of confidence.

* Likes at least some of the same things you do.

* You can trust with your secrets and worries.

* You may sometimes fall out with, but know you can probably make up with.

* Shares your values, the things that really matter to you.

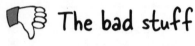 # The bad stuff

OK, so a frenemy, or toxic friend, is the total **opposite** to all those lovely things, so they are someone who:

* Won't defend you if you're in a tight spot.

* Isn't fun to spend time with, as you don't enjoy the same things.

* Betrays your trust again and again.

* Doesn't listen to you or respect your views.

* Puts you down and makes you feel on edge.

* Makes you do things you don't want to if you want to stay friends.

* Never says sorry for hurting your feelings.

* Doesn't agree with what you believe is right and wrong.

Some experts call what frenemies do 'relational aggression' (but let's call it 'being very unkind'). It's a form of bullying – which we'll look at more in the next chapter – and nobody ever deserves it.

If you have a friend who behaves in any of these ways, or makes you feel any of these bad, negative feelings, perhaps it's time to reassess your friendship – or even end it. Life's too short.

Frenemy tactics

So how do you spot a frenemy, if they are so good at hiding how nasty they really are? Here are some scenarios showing how they might behave. Reading them might help you to see how they operate:

1 You've coloured your hair. All your friends say it looks great — except one, who makes sure you see them rolling their eyes and snorting with laughter.

2 You've arranged a gaming session with three other people. Behind your back, one of them says to the others that the game you chose is 'for babies', so now nobody will play.

3 Every lunchtime, one of your group always makes sure you're the one sitting at the end of the table, so you're left out of all the chat.

4 Whenever you get a good mark in a test, one of your group always says, in a 'jokey/not jokey' way that you probably cheated, because your dad is a teacher at the school.

CHEAT!

Does any of this unkindness sound familiar? Probably, unfortunately. Frenemies are very good at doing what they do, and it can be tricky to know how to respond. If you get angry, they may say you're 'over-reacting'. If you get upset, they may say you're a wimp. But read on, because there ARE ways of fighting back at frenemies and stopping them in their tracks.

Facing a frenemy

It's not easy to challenge someone who is making you feel small, and doing it so cleverly that other people might not have even noticed. Frenemies can really make you feel bad about yourself (which true friends would never do). You might even feel like treating them as badly as they are treating you, but being unkind would probably make you feel even worse. So, what **can** you do?

If you have to face a frenemy, try some, or all, of these tactics to find out which one works for you. It's tough, and you'll need to be strong, but you know you have to try, for your own sake.

Keep your head low

Stay out of their way as much as possible. It may not solve the problem long-term, but it's a small win and could buy you some breathing space.

Ignore them

Frenemies love seeing how much they have upset you. If you don't let them see that they have, they might just lose interest. It's worth a try, if you can do it, but you'll need to be tough.

Challenge them

If you can be really firm and strong in how you react to them, frenemies won't like it at all. This is called ASSERTIVENESS (more about this on pages 188 and 189). It's not easy, but it can be learned. Go you!

You could say things like:

> Did it make you feel good to speak to me like that?

> I'm going to sit HERE today*.

> I don't want to do that. You're on your own there.

*And do it!

Spread the word

Tell other friends exactly what's going on and how it makes you feel. They may not know. Next time frenemies strike, they will, hopefully, support you.

Get help

If you are finding it really tricky to tackle someone who is making your life difficult, you must tell someone you trust, such as a parent, carer or teacher.

Stop!

Here's one last tactic to consider. Imagine you were watching someone doing all this to SOMEONE ELSE, someone you really care about? You'd want them to stop right now, wouldn't you? Remember how important it is to 'be true to you'? Well, perhaps it's time to stick up for yourself as much as you would do for someone else.

Coming soon...

The next chapter covers a much more severe version of the spitefulness of toxic friends: **bullying**. Many of the tactics in this chapter will be useful, but bullies are a whole new level of meanness. Luckily, this book is here to help you cope.

CHAPTER ELEVEN

Bullies and bullying

Bullies may not seem to belong in a book about friendship, but, like 'frenemies', they are out there, so you need to know how to deal with them. As you make friends and form relationships, you may be the victim of a bully, witness others being bullied, or even bully someone yourself. It happens, but it's

NOT acceptable, in any form, **EVER**.

This chapter will help you understand a bit more about how bullies operate, and suggest ways of keeping them out of your life.

PING PING PING

How can I get them to stop it and leave me alone?

What is bullying?

If you look in a dictionary, you'll find the word 'bullying' defined like this:

bullying

deliberate, repeated abuse by a powerful person of a less powerful one, meaning to cause them hurt or harm. Bullying can happen in person, or online.

So what kind of person would behave like this? Perhaps you're picturing a big, uber-aggressive 'alpha male' or a spiteful, hard 'queen-bee'. Well, it might surprise you to learn that very few bullies fit this stereotype. It's true that boys and girls tend to use different methods to bully people, but their nasty aim is the same: to HURT someone for no good reason at all.

Most bullies use words, rather than muscles, as weapons, but they can be just as lethal.

There's a huge amount of research into bullying and a lot of different expert opinions. You may not feel that finding out more will help you much, but *understanding* something can make it much easier to *manage* it, so let's do it.

BUT...

Always remember that you did not ask to be bullied and you don't deserve to be.

IT'S **NOT** YOUR FAULT.

Why do bullies bully?

Let's look at some of the main reasons experts give for why bullies bully:

1 It's 'natural'

Many young animals play fight, or 'flex their muscles' from time to time, to seem powerful. Chimps (yes, them again) wrestle ferociously, for example. Some experts say it's all part of growing-up.

2 Bullies are sad

Some bullies pick on people they see as weaker than they are because of problems in their own lives, or because they have been bullied themselves. Passing the misery on to someone else reduces it for them.

③ Bullies don't understand feelings

Remember the word 'empathy', that means 'the ability to understand other peoples' feelings'? Some experts believe bullies don't have much of this. Others say that bullies understand feelings very well, and know <u>exactly</u> how to hurt them. Whichever is true, what bullies do is rubbish.

④ Bullies like to lead

Some bullies enjoy having followers whom they actively encourage to witness them bullying. It makes them feel powerful and popular. They believe that nobody will dare challenge or stop them (just in case they get bullied themselves).

OK, so now you know why some people bully others. Let's find out more about how bullies and their victims tend to behave. Knowing more will help you understand, and deal with it better.

WHAT WOULD YOU DO?

You *can't* choose not to be bullied (though that would be great!), but you *can* choose how you respond to it. Let's look at how you think you'd react in these tricky situations, for instance. Answer **totally honestly**, please:

Q1 – The class bully threw your gym kit into a muddy puddle AGAIN. **WHAT WOULD YOU DO?**

a) Say nothing and wear the muddy kit anyway.

b) Tell the teacher that you're being victimized.

c) See if you can borrow some kit from lost property.

Q2 – The bully in your year has told all your mates not to speak to you as a 'joke'. **WHAT WOULD YOU DO?**

a) Put up with the silent treatment until it ends.

b) Challenge your friends and tell them to stop it.

c) Find other people to talk to for a while.

Q3 – A girl in your class always teases you about your accent in lessons. **WHAT WOULD YOU DO?**

a)   Decide not to speak at all in class. It's safer.

b)   Speak up even more. Do you really care what she thinks?

c)   Try to stay calm. It's only banter, after all.

Q4 – A boy in your class is always being bullied by a group of older kids. **WHAT WOULD YOU DO?**

a)   Ignore it, and let him fight his own battles. You have to.

b)   Stick up for the boy whenever you see him being bullied.

c)   Try to help him stay out of their way, whenever you can.

Bullies create real fear, so if you chose the a) and c) answers, that's fine. Those are the reactions most of us would choose if we're honest, but wouldn't it be great to be able to choose the b) ones*, and **face** that fear?

*If you DID choose the b) ones, by the way, good for you!

Time to talk

The first step in facing up to bullying is to **talk about it**. Bullies often rely on their victims being too scared and ashamed to tell anyone, but experts agree that talking about it is vital. If people don't know, they can't help, and telling someone will release part of your stress.

- You could start by telling just one other person, a friend on an online group, or even your diary.
- You might find that talking about it then helps you tell someone who can do something about it.
- Is there someone in your life who will listen, but not spread what you say (unless you want them to)?

Aunty, I need to talk to you.

- Talk about it with someone you trust while you're both in a car, or walking next to them. It's easier.
- Finally, you could try talking to the bully. They may not fully realize the impact of their behaviour on you.

Believe in you

The next step involves starting to believe in yourself; telling yourself that you **do** have some of the resilience and inner toughness we looked at in Chapter 9. It's not easy, but remember that bullies thrive on FEAR, so if you seem strong (even if you don't feel it), it can spoil their horrible fun.

- Walk away. However you're feeling, be strong, turn your back and go.
- Breathe slowly and deeply, to help you stay 'in the moment' and not panic.

Turn the page for more tips.

Goodbye!

- Imagine throwing their nastiness away, like a prickly cactus or a hot potato.
- Truly believe that this is not your fault, that it will end and that you WILL get through it.

Stand up for others

So, now you have some tactics for standing up for yourself when you're being bullied, BUT (and this is a bit awkward) have you ever seen someone else being bullied and not done anything to stop it? If you have, you are far from alone.

#!@$!!

Should I do something?

Research shows that many bullies rely on nobody challenging them, so one way of beating them is to do just that. Fighting back for others strengthens your self-belief, too, so it's a win-win. Experts call doing this being an 'upstander', not a 'bystander'.*

There's a bully in the group...

If you have a bully in your group of friends, it's hard to stop them on your own, but if you can work together, as a team, and work out a strategy, you're so much stronger.

Bullies thrive on all their followers being fearful of them – so don't be. Fight back, together.

*A *bystander* just watches things happening.

Online bullying

Sadly, there's another area of bullying we need to look at in this chapter: online bullying. Today, it's many bullies' weapon of choice, and it can be very hard indeed to cope with. Online bullying doesn't stop when you get home from school, and bullies can say things online that they would never, ever say to your face, because nobody is watching.

Being resilient helps, and trying not to let the bullies 'get inside your head' does too, but the reality is that you may need help with this cruel, cowardly form of bullying. It's truly horrible.

Coming up on the next page, you'll find some online bully-busting tactics to try – you may need them ALL, but that's OK.

- Sometimes, the quickest solution is to remove the bully's 'weapons', and take a break from social media. It gives you some recovery time, too.

- It's just as important to tell someone about online bullying as it is about any other kind. You need not suffer in silence. Find someone you trust, and tell them.

- If the nasty comments are from someone you know, talk to them face-to-face to find out why they are posting these things. Perhaps you can sort it together?

Of course, it takes courage to go offline for a while; you can feel as if you're missing out. But remember that going *offline* takes away an *online* bully's weapon: it means they can't reach you.

Trolling

Trolls are vicious creatures in fairy tales, and online 'trolls' are equally nasty, and yet another form of bully. In a dictionary, you will find that 'trolling' means something like this:

trolling

doing or saying something online to upset someone, get attention or cause trouble.

I like being REALLY mean!

Online trolls usually target lots of people they don't know with abuse, threats or rude stuff, to see who reacts. They hide their identity, so they can post anything, however unkind, untrue or personal. They often target celebrities, but can also pick on anyone they can connect with online – which could be YOU.

The best ways to get rid of them are to:

Block them immediately.

Not react at all and hope they go away.

Report them to the platform they used.

Are YOU a bully?

You've seen some of the reasons why bullies bully, but all of us have the potential to become a bully. If we feel cornered, or not very confident, it's all too easy to lash out at others to try to make ourselves feel a bit better, isn't it?

Which brings us to a tricky question:

Have you ever bullied anyone, deliberately making them unhappy by the way you treat them?

If your answer is '**Yes**', well done for saying so.

Acknowledging it can be the first step in *stopping* it. If you are worried about what you are doing, talk to someone you trust, who cares about you. They will guide you towards further help. You may need some counselling, to understand *why* you are bullying, but the first step is to accept that you *need* that help. That is a very brave step indeed.

Help is out there

Hopefully, you will never be bullied or be a bully yourself, but you may see it, or hear about it, so it's important you understand it. This chapter has suggested lots of ways of standing up to bullies.

There's no avoiding the fact they all take real courage, but the more brave people that DO say "STOP", the sooner the bullies will be beaten.

Bullying is a form of abuse, and nobody should have to endure it. If you are being bullied, you must ask for help. Do not feel you have to suffer in silence: **tell someone**.

Most schools have anti-bullying policies and members of staff whose responsibility is to tackle bullying in all its forms. There are lots of anti-bullying websites, online chats and helplines for you to contact. The sad fact that so many people, of all ages, are bullied means that there is a huge amount of help out there, so use it.*

Finally, remember that you are a worthwhile, cherished person, and deserve to be happy. Your family and your friends would want that, too.

CHAPTER TWELVE

The same, but different

> You are one hundred per cent unique, a complete one-off, an individual. There is nobody exactly like you anywhere else in the whole world.

Do you remember reading that, way back at the beginning of this book?

Well, it's still true: each one of us *is* different in lots of ways, but have you ever thought about how *alike* we all are, in many others? In this chapter, we'll focus on what we have in common with other people, and how our attitudes to each other can sometimes limit our friendship choices.

I am who I am

We are all products of our upbringing, our backgrounds, our society, our peers and our education – whether we like it or not. We can take new ideas on board and change in many ways as we go through life, but we can't change that starting point: it's where we came from.

 Sometimes, this can mean that we see the world, and other people, through a bit of a limited lens (think of it as one side of a pair of binoculars, if you like). However hard we try, seeing the *whole* picture is not always easy, but being aware of that is a very good start.

So, we know that it's good to share interests and values with our mates and to have a good time together, but what about people whom you might not see as 'instant friend material', because the differences between you seem too big to overcome?

Have you ever become friends with someone you never imagined you would when you first met? If you have, you'll know what a good feeling it can be. With friendship, it's worth trying to think outside the box...

I'm so glad we took a chance on each other.

See, don't judge

Sometimes, you just *know* that someone is too different for you two to become friends. Perhaps the girl in your drama class is too loud, or the captain of the football team is too full of himself? That's fine: you can't be friends with everyone, but we often make up our minds about other people in *seconds*. We judge them on what they look like, how they speak, what they are wearing and lots of other tiny 'signals'. **But we can be, and often are, wrong.**

Looking at differences

The world is full of different kinds of people and different ways of living. It's vital that we notice our differences, and celebrate them, but it's just as important that we see our similarities and the things we all share.

You could compare the huge variety in our society to an amazing fruit salad in which each individual ingredient is needed to create something delicious. This is what is often called 'diversity', a word you probably know. Put very simply, it means:

diversity

a wide range, which includes all kinds of different people, animals and plants.

To help you have as wide a choice of friends as you can, it's worth taking a closer look at some of the differences between people, so that you can decide how important they are to you. Some differences are bigger than others.

The BIG ones

These big differences can be the hardest ones to get past, but the rewards for doing so are equally big. We learn a lot about the world from others, so the more 'others' you meet, the better. Here are some of them:

family background

sexuality gender

beliefs religion culture

physical ability language

age

Some smaller ones

As every single one of us is different, there are bound to be **lots** of ways that no two people are the same. Here are just a few:

- How we speak (our accent or language)
- How we dress (our style)
- What we like to eat (and what we don't)
- Our hopes for the future
- Our opinions about issues such as climate change
- Our tastes in music
- Our skills, strengths and weaknesses

Tiny ones

...and finally, there are EVEN MORE tiny differences between each and every one of us. Here are a few:

- The precise colour of our eyes
- The exact sound of our voice
- The way we laugh
- The shape of our big toenails
- How we eat a sandwich

Differences are there, all around us, but they need not get in the way of friendship. They are part of life and they make life so much richer, for all of us.

A friend is a friend

Small children are the experts at seeing and accepting difference. Diversity comes naturally to them, because a friend is a friend, whatever their skin colour, religion, sex, or age. They have no 'friendship filter', rather like some animals. And how many videos have you watched where a dog becomes besties with a cat, or a rabbit won't leave a horse's side? Be honest, folks. It all sounds great, but where do you fit in?

Well, you're in luck, because your generation is probably more open-minded than any previous generation of young people. In many parts of the world, diversity is acknowledged, discussed and actively celebrated. People are allowed to express themselves far more freely than even a decade ago.*

*Sadly this is not yet the case everywhere, but let's hope things improve in the future.

Let's try an experiment:

Can you think of someone you know a bit, quite like, but are not sure whether you can be friends with them because you don't seem very alike? Without thinking too hard, jot down all the things you have in common, however small, on a piece of paper.

Start with the basics, if you like, such as 'we're both boys', 'we both have brown eyes', or 'we both live in the same town'. It doesn't need to be complex. Here are a few examples to help you get started:

- **We both have a brother.**

- **We both have black hair.**

- **Both our mums work at home.**

- **We both enjoy gaming after school.**

- **We're both quite shy.**

- **We both like rap.**

- **We both go bowling.**

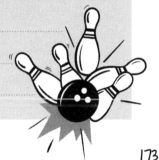

Your list could go on for AGES, as there are probably loads of things you have in common with any other person roughly your age if you think hard enough.

Now, jot down what you see as the differences between you:

- I am better at Maths than you are.

- You wear glasses. I don't.

- I go to a temple. You go to a church.

- We live in a bigger house than you do.

- You have a dog. We don't.

- You play the guitar. I play the clarinet.

- Your dad is Irish. My dad is Pakistani.

- I wear a head-covering. You don't.

Yes, we have differences.

But SO WHAT?

Do you think any of these things would stop you at least trying to be friends? It may work, it may not, but remember that we discovered earlier in this book that a friend is a person who shares your interests and values, is fun to spend time with, and has your back if things get tough.
If THOSE things 'click', a friendship can grow, whatever your differences.

People can be full of surprises, and friendships form in the unlikeliest of circumstances. Why not push the boundaries a little?

Bridging the gaps

This chapter has looked at an area of friendship that you may not have thought about before – how we decide who to be friends with without even realizing we're doing it. Hopefully, now you'll see similarities rather than differences when you meet someone who is not exactly like you, and look through *both* sides of those binoculars.

Sometimes it's not easy, but if you can, why not be an ambassador for diversity, and give everyone you meet a chance?

Let's be friends.

CHAPTER THIRTEEN

The best of friends

So, you've learned a lot about friends, and how important they are for your wellbeing and happiness. Friends are as important as your family or carers (and may feel *more* important at times). They are the people you grow up with, learn from, feel closest to, have adventures with... and probably make lots of mistakes with, too.

You've also discovered that friendship is complex, and that there's LOADS of research about it.

For instance, some experts think you need lots of different kinds of friends. Others say that a few close ones are better, and a few think that one really good mate is enough. There's no 'one size fits all' when it comes to friendship, so never worry that you're getting it wrong. Some of us need one thing, and some another, because we are all different. The main thing is to make sure your friends are people:

* You can trust, always, with anything.

* Who respect and care about you.

* Who will treat you with kindness.

...and remember that you need to do JUST THE SAME for them! Friendship is a two-way thing.

What you know now

Here's a checklist of the main aspects of friends and friendship you've already looked at:

- ☑ **Why we need friends.**
- ☑ **What makes a good friend.**
- ☑ **How friendships can begin.**
- ☑ **The pros and cons of besties.**
- ☑ **How to cope with gangs and cliques.**
- ☑ **Tips for keeping frenemies at bay.**
- ☑ **Managing fall-outs with mates.**
- ☑ **Tactics for beating bullying.**
- ☑ **How to make as wide a range of friends as you can.**

Great stuff. But there are two more things that are SO important, they really are worth exploring further. Read on...

Liking yourself.

Staying true to you.

Looking a little more closely at these two areas, you'll see how much they affect you and all your friendships. You'll find some useful tips to guide you, too.

How to like yourself

Remember jotting down four good things about yourself? Like many people, you may have found that difficult, because it touches on how much you actually *like* yourself. This is called your **self-esteem**, and it's at the heart of healthy friendships. If your self-esteem is a bit wobbly, other people pick up on it, and may even buy into the 'negative you' you are putting across. Don't let that happen. If you're not sure whether you like yourself much (and you are *not* alone if that's so) you can actually *learn* to – honestly! Here's how...

When you're alone, say something POSITIVE about yourself out loud. (It's important that you say it, rather than write it down this time.) If you can, stand in front of a mirror to do it, as that's even more powerful. You might say something like:

'Learning to like yourself' may sound a bit weird, but it's an approach to caring for ourselves that's becoming popular as more and more people struggle with anxiety, stress and low confidence.

Strong, positive statements like these are called **affirmations**. You may not find them easy to say at first, but it will get easier. Saying good things about yourself really helps you start to believe them. In time, they may pop into your head just when you need a shot of self-confidence.

My opinions matter.

TIP TWO | GO EASY ON YOURSELF

Don't compare yourself to others, in life or on social media platforms. Young people can feel huge pressure to be 'perfect', and a massive sense of inadequacy if they think they're not. Glamorous models, rich celebrities and 'cool' influencers are everywhere, and it can be easy to feel that you should to be just as slim/fit/buff/successful/rich as they are, but let's take a closer look...

Firstly, remember that influencers and celebs probably have a team of stylists, a massive wardrobe and a mega budget. It's their JOB.

Secondly, many photos online are edited, filtered, airbrushed and tweaked. THEY ARE NOT REAL.

Finally, how many of these people are truly happy and have strong, loving relationships? There's more to life than thousands of followers. Just sayin'.

So go easy on yourself, and try not to set yourself standards of perfection that NOBODY can possibly reach. Remember the term 'inner critic'? Well that little voice inside your head can be very persuasive, but it's important to give yourself some self-love and to tell yourself that you probably AREN'T *perfect* (who really is, with the filters off?) but that:

You ARE just as good as anyone else.

Another powerful tool in 'learning to like yourself' is gratitude (being grateful). Whenever you can, try to:

Be grateful for the good stuff.

There will always be parts of your life that you wish were different, but try to be grateful for the things you DO like (however small they seem). Also, remember the people who care about you and be grateful for them. Even your Aunty Flora.

Jot down a list of these good things, run through them in your head, or say 'thank you' out loud when nobody's around – it doesn't matter which. The point is to make you look at the positive rather than the negative side of yourself and your life. If you see it, and believe in it, others will too.

I am grateful for...
- Mr Sniffles
- carrot cake
- TJ and Joe

Remember that every single one of us has doubts, dips in self-confidence and moments of feeling that nobody else understands us. If you try as hard as you can to be a friend to *yourself*, others are likely to see that, respect you and want to be your friend. Some people call this 'being happy in your own skin', which sounds good, doesn't it? Why not give it a try?

Staying true to you

Being able to be your true self with your mates is one of the best things about friendship, but this can be tested at times. Remember the idea of core values, or 'the beliefs that really matter to you'? You made a list of four of them and thought about how important it is to stay true to them. It sounds easy, but it isn't easy AT ALL when you're up against it. The next few tips will help you 'stay true to you'.

Sometimes, you may well disagree with something friends want to do, or think is OK. The pressure to do what everyone else is doing (peer pressure), can be hard to resist. If you find yourself in this situation, you need to express your views in a calm but firm way, without making your mates feel judged. This is called **being assertive**. To speak up at times like these, try saying things like:

Another useful assertiveness tip is to use what is sometimes called 'the broken record technique'*. All you have to do is to say what you think calmly and clearly, as before, but keep saying it until your friends have heard you. It sounds simple, and it is – but it can be very effective!

Let's go into town after school.

I think we should go on Saturday. We've got so much homework.

We won't stay long. It'll be fun.

No, let's go on Saturday. I want to do my homework tonight.

Let's just go for an hour or so. Come on.

I'm not going today. We'll enjoy it more on Saturday.

TIP SIX   CHOOSE YOUR TRIBE

Another way of making sure you stay true to yourself is to surround yourself with like-minded people, who see the world the way you do. If you do so, you're *less* likely to make different choices and *more* likely to want the same things. There are exceptions, of course, but it's a sound general rule.

*The name is from vinyl records that sometimes stick and play the same thing again and again!

If you're quite shy, for example, you might feel over-shadowed by a loud, super-confident friend. If you're a computer nerd, you're more likely to click with another one than with someone who hates gaming.

This doesn't mean that we can't be friends with different kinds of people, or that a vegan can never be mates with a meat-eater. Far from it, BUT it's much easier to stay true to yourself if those around you respect, if not actually share, most of your core values.

You're sure we can be friends?

But remember, people can surprise you. Try to give everyone a chance, even if you don't seem alike at first.

Of course.

TIP SEVEN | BE YOUR BEST SELF

The final part of your 'being true to you' is to keep remembering to show others your best self. This isn't always easy, as not everyone is kind or thoughtful, but if YOU are, you can always feel proud of yourself. Experts say that we tend to treat others as we have been treated ourselves, so if you want **kind** and **thoughtful** mates, you'd better:

- **Be one yourself!**
- **Choose friends wisely. Good ones can make all the difference in your life.**
- **Cherish your friends. Listen to them and give them support if they need it.**
- **Chill with your friends. Life can be stressful, so enjoy the chance to relax and be yourself.**

And finally...

- **Be a friendship CHAMP, by being the very best friend you can be.**

Glossary

app (application)
software designed to run on a mobile device

assertive
being able to state your views clearly and calmly

bullying
deliberate, repeated abuse by a powerful person
of a less powerful one

clique
a small group of people who often make others
feel unwelcome

diversity
a wide range, which includes all kinds of different
people, things, animals and plants

empathy
the ability to understand and share another
person's feelings

endorphins
chemicals released by the brain that can make
you feel happier

FOMO
fear of missing out

frenemy
someone who is not a real friend (and more like an enemy)

groupthink
what happens when a group of people all think and believe the same thing

inner critic
an imagined voice inside your head that criticizes you and makes you feel bad

meme
something posted on social media that's usually funny and is widely shared

notification
an alert telling you of a new message, post or update

peer
a person who is in roughly the same situation in life as you are

peer pressure
pressure to fit in with others around you and do what they are doing

resilience

inner strength, or toughness, which helps you get through difficult times

self-esteem

confidence in yourself and your value as a person

self-love

giving yourself small treats, to make yourself feel good

social media

online sites and apps that you can use to share ideas or contact people

toxic friend

an unkind friend who does not have your best interests at heart

trolling

posting something hurtful or rude online to make someone else miserable

validation

accepting that someone is valuable and that their views are worthwhile

Index

Notes

Here are some of the other books in this series:

Editorial assistance from
Alice Beecham

First published in 2023 by Usborne Publishing Limited,
83-85 Saffron Hill, London EC1N 8RT, United Kingdom.

usborne.com

Printed in the UK. UKE.